# Chris Colfer

ABDO
Publishing Company

Big Buddy BOOKS
Buddy Bios

by **Sarah Tieck**

## VISIT US AT
### www.abdopublishing.com

Published by ABDO Publishing Company, PO Box 398166, Minneapolis, Minnesota 55439.

Copyright © 2014 by Abdo Consulting Group, Inc. International copyrights reserved in all countries. No part of this book may be reproduced in any form without written permission from the publisher. Big Buddy Books™ is a trademark and logo of ABDO Publishing Company.

Printed in the United States of America, North Mankato, Minnesota.
052013
092013

 PRINTED ON RECYCLED PAPER

Coordinating Series Editor: Rochelle Baltzer
Contributing Editors: Megan M. Gunderson, Marcia Zappa
Graphic Design: Maria Hosley
Cover Photograph: *AP Photo*: Jordan Strauss/Invision.
Interior Photographs/Illustrations: *AP Photo*: Ross D. Franklin (p. 13), Little Brown & Co. Children's Books (p. 27), Chris Pizzello (pp. 5, 16), FOX, Adam Rose, File (p. 15), Matt Sayles (pp. 17, 25), Dan Steinberg/Invision (p. 19), Jordan Strauss/Invision (p. 17), Donald Traill (p. 23); *Getty Images*: Paul Archuleta/FilmMagic (p. 21), Anthony Behar/Bravo/NBCU Photo Bank via Getty Images (p. 11), Munawar Hosain/Fotos International (p. 9), Ilya S. Savenok/WireImage (p. 28), Amy Sussman/Getty Images for Fox (p. 12), Kevin Winter (p. 7).

### Library of Congress Control Number: 2012956010

### Cataloging-in-Publication Data

Tieck, Sarah.
 Chris Colfer: star of Glee / Sarah Tieck.
  p. cm. -- (Big buddy biographies)
 ISBN 978-1-61783-857-6
 1. Colfer, Chris, 1990- --Juvenile literature. 2. Actors--United States--Biography--Juvenile literature. 3. Singers--United States--Biography--Juvenile literature. I. Title.
 791.4302--dc23
 [B]                                                     2012956010

Chris Colfer

# Contents

# Rising Star

Chris Colfer is a talented actor and singer. He is also an author. He is best known as one of the stars of the television show *Glee*.

Chris plays Kurt Hummel on *Glee*.

5

Oregon

California Nevada

PACIFIC OCEAN

Fresno

Arizona

MEXICO

# Family Ties

Christopher Paul "Chris" Colfer was born in Fresno, California, on May 27, 1990. Chris's parents are Karyn and Tim Colfer. His sister is Hannah.

Chris grew up in nearby Clovis, California. His family was very supportive. Hannah has a health condition that causes **seizures**. Chris helped care for her and they became close.

Sometimes, Hannah attends events with Chris.

# Early Years

From a young age, Chris knew he wanted to be an actor. He played Snoopy in a local play at age eight! His parents and others noticed his natural talent.

Chris worked hard to build his dream. In high school, he wrote, directed, and starred in a play.

Chris's family supported his dream of working as an actor.

# Facing Bullies

In high school, Chris was **bullied**. Other students said unkind things and made fun of him. Even though they never hurt his body, their words hurt his feelings.

Chris says the students picked on him for a variety of reasons. He said it was mainly because he was different than they were. Chris overcame this by going into his mind and making plans for his **future**.

Chris has talked about bullying with reporters. In 2012, *Glee* costars Jane Lynch (*left*), Cory Monteith (*second from right*), and Lea Michele (*right*) joined him.

Fans and cast members make the "L" sign with their hands to show they like *Glee*.

Sometimes the cast sings for live audiences. Some of these performances were used in *Glee: The 3D Concert Movie* in 2011.

# Big Break

At age 18, Chris tried out for *Glee*. He got his first television role! He was very excited. *Glee* started airing in 2009. It became popular very quickly. *Glee* is a musical television show about a singing group, or glee club. It is both funny and serious. The show began when the characters were in high school. Many, such as Kurt, have graduated but are still on the show.

Chris plays Kurt Hummel on *Glee*. On the
show, Kurt is **bullied** because he is gay.
He stands up for himself. Some people say
Chris's acting has helped teach people to
respect each other's differences.

Chris works closely with Darren Criss on *Glee*. Darren plays Blaine Anderson. Kurt and Blaine were a couple on the show.

# Award Winner

People have honored Chris's acting talent with important awards. In 2010, Chris won a Teen Choice Award for being a scene stealer. In 2012, he won another for acting in a **comedy**.

In 2011, Chris won a Golden Globe Award for best supporting actor on a television show. In 2013, he won a People's Choice Award for favorite TV comedy actor.

Chris's work on *Glee* has been honored with awards. These include Teen Choice Awards (*left*), a Golden Globe Award (*center*), and a People's Choice Award (*right*).

17

# New Directions

Chris's talent and hard work have earned him more opportunities. One area is in writing. Chris has written stories, novels, and **screenplays** for television and movies. In 2012, Chris starred in a movie he had written. It is called *Struck By Lightning*.

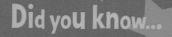

**Did you know...**

In 2011, Chris spent time working on a screenplay of the book *The Little Leftover Witch*. He hoped it would become a Disney television show someday.

Rebel Wilson acted in *Struck By Lightning* with Chris.

## Did you know...

In high school, Chris was the editor of his school's writing magazine!

*Struck by Lightning* is about high school students who work on a school writing magazine. Chris took some ideas from his own high school experiences for the story. But, most of the movie's events are made up.

After *Struck By Lightning* came out, Chris wrote a book based on the movie. It tells more of the story.

# An Actor's Life

When *Glee* is filming, Chris works on **set** for several hours each day. He spends time practicing **lines** and **performing**. Because *Glee* is a **musical**, Chris also practices singing and dancing.

Sometimes, the cast of *Glee* travels to film shows. In 2011, they filmed in Central Park in New York City, New York.

23

As an actor, Chris attends events and meets fans. Sometimes fans ask for autographs and pictures. Chris also appears on television shows and talks to reporters.

*Glee* fans are sometimes called "Gleeks."

# Off the Screen

When Chris is not working, he spends time with his family and friends. He also enjoys writing. In 2012, Chris's novel for children came out. It is called *The Land of Stories: The Wishing Spell*.

Chris likes to help others, too. Some of his work with *Glee* has raised awareness and money for causes. These include groups that help people in countries such as Ethiopia.

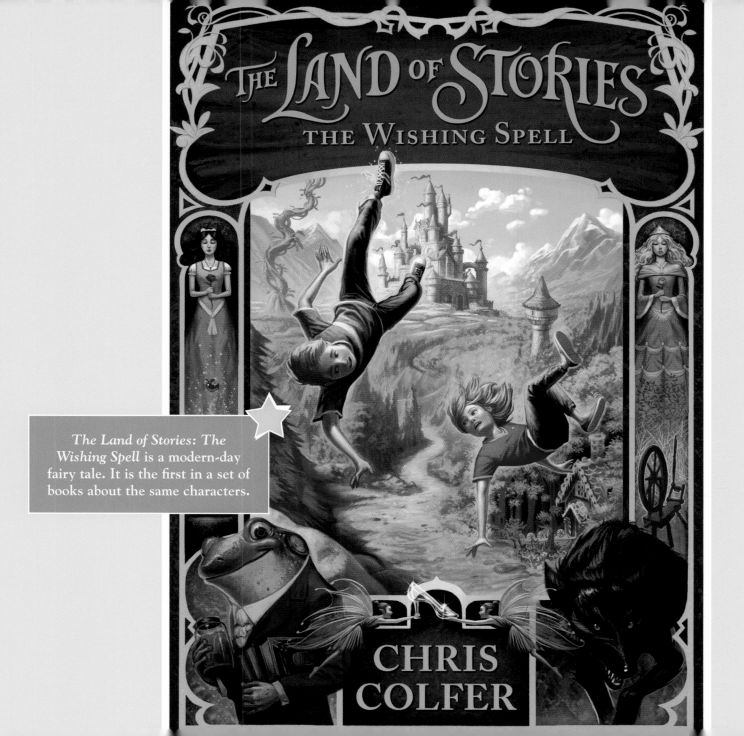

# THE LAND OF STORIES
## THE WISHING SPELL

*The Land of Stories: The Wishing Spell* is a modern-day fairy tale. It is the first in a set of books about the same characters.

# CHRIS COLFER

Chris works hard on his ideas and goals.

# Buzz

Chris's fame continues to grow. In 2013, Chris appeared on *Glee*'s fourth season. He also spent time working on the next Land of Stories novel.

Fans look forward to what's next for Chris! Many believe he has a bright **future**.

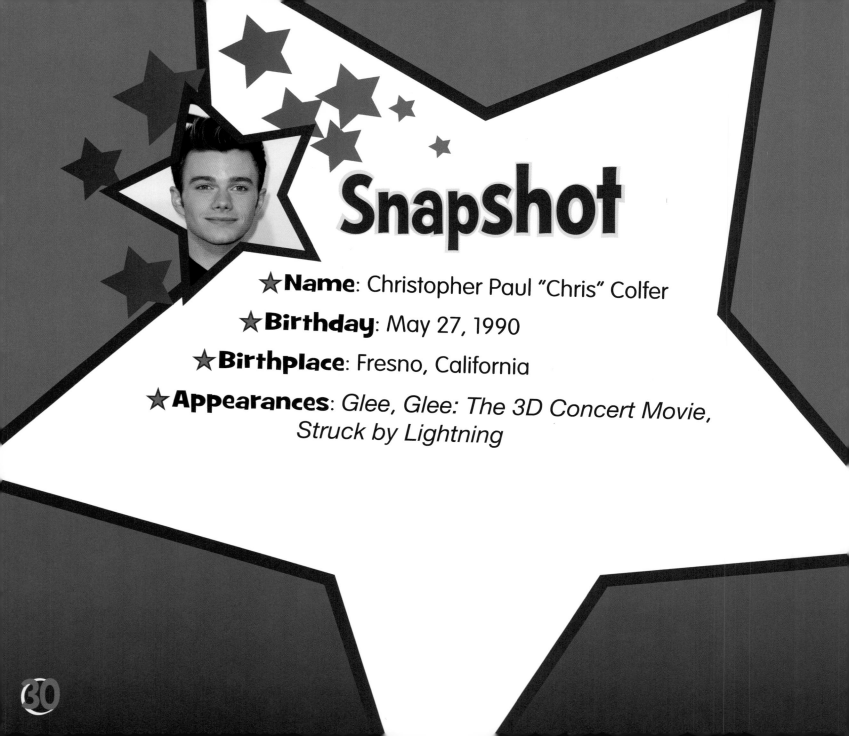

# Snapshot

★**Name**: Christopher Paul "Chris" Colfer

★**Birthday**: May 27, 1990

★**Birthplace**: Fresno, California

★**Appearances**: *Glee, Glee: The 3D Concert Movie, Struck by Lightning*

# Important Words

**air** to show on television or play on the radio.

**bully** to tease, hurt, or frighten someone.

**comedy** a funny story.

**future** (FYOO-chuhr) a time that has not yet occurred.

**graduate** (GRA-juh-wayt) to complete a level of schooling.

**lines** the words an actor says in a play, a movie, or a show.

**musical** a story told with music.

**perform** to do something in front of an audience.

**role** a part an actor plays.

**screenplay** the written text for a movie, which includes instructions for the actors and film crew.

**seizure** (SEE-zhuhr) the physical signs, such as shaking and loss of body control, of a brain disorder.

**set** the place where a movie or a television show is recorded.

# Web Sites

To learn more about Chris Colfer, visit ABDO Publishing Company online. Web sites about Chris Colfer are featured on our Book Links page. These links are routinely monitored and updated to provide the most current information available.

## www.abdopublishing.com

# Index